D1453732

How to Wear This Body

Also by Hayden Saunier

Tips for Domestic Travel
Say Luck
Field Trip to the Underworld (chapbook)

How to Wear
This Body

by

Hayden Saunier

*to Betsey and Madeleine
with best wishes –
Hayden Saunier
5/17/18*

Terrapin Books

Terrapin Books
4 Midvale Avenue
West Caldwell, NJ 07006

www.terrapinbooks.com

ISBN: 978-0-9976666-9-4
LCCN: 2017940738

First Edition

Cover art by Hayden Saunier

Contents

4

I am this body and the weather all year round.

—Philip Schultz, "Like Wings"

1

Performing Heart Repair Surgery at 2 A.M.
While Asleep

See, there's no blood.
The skin is a smooth waxy placket

that softly unbuttons.
Your breastbone splits neat

as a squeeze-open coin purse,
which is lucky because your terror of knives,

their cold shine
and quickness, their proof that time travels in only one way

hasn't slammed shut the dream doors
allowing your hands to hold your chest wide

as you sit up in bed
and dump out the small frightened fist

that's your heart
in your lap.

No surprise here.
You remember each scar, every mend, bite, and sizeable

chunk torn away or cut out,
shoveled back, re-attached, re-inflated,

but what makes you gasp
are the tools you've kept stashed, and their weight,

falling out of your chest—pocket knife, pliers,
a glue gun, two shrimp forks, electrical tape,

black *and* yellow, wire snips, needles and twine—
just in case, just in case, you need them again.

No wonder hearts hammer their hurts at the dark water margins
of sleep—it's the weight of repair over years

and this lightness
you feel once you lift your heart

back into place, seal your bones,
smooth your skin: that's the dream.

Hard Facts (My Cat)

My cat's not coming back.
Coyotes need to feed
their pups, the red-tail steady
on the storm-struck oak,
her chicks. However civilized
it looks out there among
our salmon pink geraniums
edged with dwarf lobelia's
cobalt blue, the mint sends
creeping rhizomes underneath
this turning earth each day
to crack the mortar between
farmhouse stones and take us
down. The creek's dead low,
breeds golden flies that feed
on blood. The cat was fourteen,
white-tipped, tiger-striped,
and never missed a meal.
All night, the barred owls
call: *Who cooks for you?*

How It Is with My Father

One good hour, then long days adrift—no rudder,
paddle, outboard, sail—the narrow beds

docked, each in its own tidy berth.
There's nothing to do but be here.

Sometimes, he finds his long length stretched out
in a canoe on the Chickahominy River,

bright sky above the gunwales, sawgrass
brushing the hull, sometimes in the skiff

his father rowed out to the big ships as a boy.
Always he's tethered.

As are we, alongside, watching
his hands worry the sheets.

We don't know which knots he needs to untie—
bowline, clove hitch, sheet bend, square—

if his hands hold the bitter end
or the working end of the line, or what forces

hold him—wind, current, tide.
All we know is: his hands were the hands that held us.

Bitter Night in the Country

Requisite dog bark. Far off.
No response.
Unless the sound of someone hammering
a plank into place counts as dialogue.
Late night fence mending
or a crime of passion,
could go either way.
But for now it's dogs and chores
and breath in clouds,
geese grieving overhead,
a lost tribe beating their wings
through unpunctuated blackness.
Crying exhaustion, hunger, fear,
they circle slowly to touch down
on the lightless earth they've longed for
where they'll settle in the meadow
and contentedly foul it for us all.

Fox Cry

A pre-verbal corner of my bone marrow
has found voice tonight,

but needing certainty I send a narrow beam of light
into the soybean field above the barn,

catch eyeshine, quick turn, liquid stride,
one pointed backward look

at my single piercing eye.
Another cry.

Riverside Attractions/Terminal Avenue

—Interstate 95 exit sign

Look how tired the river is of living.
Gone gray with it. We turn off the highway
and head for the rides near the docks
and other worn-down points of arrival and departure

on the day you get your diagnosis
which you say is every day for everyone,
and yes, you are right, but not always
so *literally*, I reply.

We stand by the river, its wide bed choked
with broken keels dragged bit by bit to the sea.
Long love will wear a body down.
But not as fast as no love will.

From the gondola cage of a half-lit Ferris wheel,
we watch sparks crackle across the bumper cars'
electric sky. We begin to rise and fall.
Our faces glow beneath rosy lights

that flicker with the sound of a calliope.
Yes, everything is coming to an end.
The way it does each hour of each day.
No better night for carnivals, you say.

Adage

Wild brambles at field's edge
hold us together. Tangle of sharpness,
needle-pointed, precise—don't
try to fight through the coiled fence
of every cautionary tale you were ever told.
Patience favors the patient.
Low clouds today. Still.
Reliable, the way a place goes quiet
ahead of cold fronts and long-predicted deaths.

Snowblower

At first, it seemed, the neighbor
had simply leaned back like a child
into a snowdrift of his own making

to look up into the warming sky.
Silence now. No more fantastic
ostrich plumes of snow arching

overhead, no teacups rattling
on kitchen hooks. Kill-switch
pulled, bright red machinery

stowed in a back shed.
His last turn carved sheer snow
cliffs down the walk, opening

to a panicked muddle
where everyone gathered around him
at the end. This, too, gone

in a few days. Already, twin tracks
of the gurney wheels disappearing
into soft tufts of dormant fescue.

Small Wish for Last Breaths

May the rag-scraps
that scour
your half-
collapsed
passageways

burnish
and polish
the last
of your light
into shine.

Her Eulogy, As If Composed by the Moon

She wrote of me often in her journal but not once
was I the same moon, always a moon particular

to each odd day and moment, the way
earth never seems the same to me, its storms

and lights and desert ranges on a spinning ride
so different night to night. She paid attention.

She saw me upside-down and ragged-edged,
spilled out, featureless, serene; she told me stories,

read me things she wrote in which I don't appear
and yet it's clear I'm there. She had a knack for that.

She even liked me gibbous, more-than-half,
that moon most people gaze up toward

then quickly turn away from, disappointed
in a moon that's fallen short.

She sat out with me on those nights too.
She'd smooth her apron, let me fill

her lap with light, or she'd rise and stand
inside the velvet thickness of the shadows that I threw.

Waxed or waning, daylit, bright, she knew me
whole and changeable, no matter what you see.

I think that might be love. Or ought to be.

2

Hard Facts (Do Not Resist)

To stay alive *do not resist*
that's what you're told

as if it were a simple act to make yourself
be only meat

and bone
pressed down into an asphalt street

and not a form of suicide
erase yourself be dead enough

that he or she or they'll decide
there is no need to kill you

though *do not resist*
can make no guarantee of this

but if you stay alive
do not resist will mean you have to stand

your dead self up
walk out into the world alive

which is another kind of death
and harder every single time

you have to kill yourself enough
(do not resist) to stay alive.

That Winter

I labored at life like it was a hard-edged
thing: grim, separate. All winter it snowed.

Details piled up, erased other details,
world gone blank and full of bright cold

packed to the horizon with its scaffold
of trees and stars and the nightly scar-sound

of huge plows scraping the iced roads raw.
Some years are like that. Spikes strapped to my feet,

I shoveled, chipped, kept my eyes fixed
to one narrow treacherous path,

while the inky plume of my dog's tail
wrote her own story into every blank field.

Deep Run

Ice-shuttered, the creek
changes course under cover,
scratches out a new path
grain by granite grain.

I stop at the crossing,
try to enter that privacy.

This doesn't last long.
I'm restless, human.
I twist every moment toward me.

The world is colder today
than my desire
to be like a stream:
to make my way
around what's insoluble,
polish sharp into smooth,
pebble to sand,
be both body and bed,
particle and wave,
no matter the weather,
but even as I say it
I know I'm the stone,
not the water.
I'm always the stone.

Nostalgia

In order to venture further into this day's
compulsive attempt to order the world
and shoehorn it into words, I've applied
a pomegranate beeswax lip balm
with natural beetroot color to my lips.
Any chapstick works, but why not juice
it up with honeybees and carmine, no one cares.
Anything can happen when the weather
blows emotional. High winds and sudden
drops in barometric pressure stir old
vocabularies out of dust and certain words
like trapdoors swing wide open, fly off,
ripped from hinges by F-4 tornados,
leave me crouched down in a howling
cellar corner, promising the gods of screech
and shrapnel anything they want to make it
stop. In times like these, I reach back
into my store of recollections for a green idea
that conjures up July's feathered grasses
brushing childhood's fingertips, the air
pungent with each meadow mint-crushed
step and there, around the next thought's
corner, is my mother in her kitchen,
sunlit, as she was when I was ten. Why
contemplate the present when the past
is right there, ready to be tarted up to suit
the mood? Sure, the lip balm helps
with chapping but it mostly makes me lick
my lips and feel the edges of the words
that tell a spell, the one that sends me back
to days and doorways where I start and

never end, before what happened
happened, everyone alive and young and
soft-lipped, tasting grains of salt and sugar
from each other's unscarred skin.

Dear T, Who Overdosed

Thanks for the bone dry slice of bread
I find deep in the pocket of my good wool coat
as I walk into church for a wedding

which I pretty much miss as I sit
in a hard Protestant pew thinking why
on earth I have bread in my good coat pocket

until I remember your funeral lunch,
three months ago, was it, or two? No appetite then,
but I took the bread because I knew

my body would eventually knock
on its own door, ask to be fed, and now it all comes back:
how no one knew to look for you

so four days passed, that part so bad all else
seemed comic, the way the undertakers never
get the mouth right on a corpse, or how

they spun your coffin in a circle like the wind-up
to a magic trick before they rolled you out,
your ex-wife in her stupid hat sobbing

in an empty row, and no, I never ate the bread
and who the hell gets married at the blunt
dead end of winter, bitterness dragged inside,

our bodies buttoned tight against the cold?
But thanks, my friend, for this bit of bread I throw out
for the churchyard birds and for reminding

me how to wear this body and this same black coat
to funerals and wedding feasts, to leave
its weight and satin lining slumped across a chair,

and every chance I get to rise and dance
in my stocking feet and fill my mouth
with wine and pure white sugar cake.

Snow after Snow

Under hemlocks, half-moons of melt
where deer bedded down, curled

bodies heating cold earth. All night,
they pass under our windows,

leave single-file paths through spring
snowfall, their startles and sidesteps

spelled out in shiny black pinecones of scat
sunk in white. Restless and hollowed

by winter, we break trail for each other,
step easily into each other's steps.

I follow the hearts of their hoofprints
to pockets of leaves they've nosed up

where I breathe in their prophesy of soften
and root down, rise up and green.

Asparagus

A first few
shoots emerge,
maroon
and aubergine
but from the start
this year, their numbers
fall away.

And so the day
we knew would come
has come.
The bed has spent itself
exactly as it's meant
to do.

But oh, the slender
multitudes we knelt beside
on damp spring afternoons,
sliced expertly with silver knives

and ate bright green
with sea salt,
threads of glossy
olive oil, back
then so many
we could never
taste the end.

Dear Friend Since Childhood

Let's set the scene
        one hour before sunset
                memory's golden hour
        light shot across the field
bright haze of pollen
        shimmering insects
                swallows dropping in and out of sky
        above the pasture's
twenty-seven different shades
        of iridescent green
                we counted once—
        we counted everything.
Let's spread those blankets out
        across tall grasses
                where our mothers sit
        barelegged, straight-backed
impossibly young
        peeling waxy opaque paper
                from chicken salad sandwiches
        or shelling hard boiled eggs
with oval fingernails
        their beautiful hands
                so fluid and cool—offering
        each other coffee from
a Scotch plaid thermos.
                Quick, dam up the creek bed
                        make a shallow pool
        the way we used to do
and lie back in the water
        kick hard against the dam
                of earth and stone
        one kick was all it ever took—

and then let's try to love
the way the current tries
to carry us away.

Hard Facts (Vengeance)

I feel his spinal column crack
beneath my feet, his cheekbones snap
and plow-blade through the spongy
grey-pink tissue of his frontal lobe,
then I get distracted figuring out how
I'll scrape what's left of him off my good shoes
onto a curb at 88th near Broadway
and since this is my revenge fantasy
why the hell don't I start out wearing boots?
I've tried many film noir variations—
(elbow-to-windpipe or grab-the-knife,
stab back repeatedly) but that's as far
as I ever get with revenge. I rough-chop
vegetables instead, make something real,
like soup. Hate's way too intimate.

A Stab at an Inkling of a Theory

Evergreen trees have it all figured out:
dress modestly, take losses daily,
keep a little darkness always at your core.
That way the end's a soft fall into snow.

Deciduous trees are far less stoic.
The woods are a crowd scene
packed with sugar maple drama queens
upstaging one another until this year's

leaves blow down and each tree strikes
its individual pose of regret and desolation,
holds it, shivering, all winter long for every eye
to see. Well, here I go again.

As though this terror at the core
belongs to anything but me.

Lament

No matter what I tap against
this blue-glazed earthen bowl bequeathed me
by a friend

(and I've tried chopsticks, sharpies,
kitchen scissors, serving spoons,
and every kind of pen),

I only hear dull thuds.
Nothing remotely
like a chime, a bell, a ring.

And yet she said that's why she bought it,
why she wanted me to have it
after she was gone—

because it sang.

And now she's gone.
And now I have it.
And I cannot make it sing.

I clear away
my clatter, leave the smooth
blue emptiness centered in the room.

It takes its time.
Like grief.

Then a low note,
an opening hum.

3

14 Degrees Below Zero in the Grocery Store Parking Lot

A dog and I stare at each other
from our separate cars, waiting for our people to return.
He's a shepherd mix, big head, big ears,
like me, he's riding shotgun.

Heat blares inside my car,
exhaust plumes from the pickup truck he's in,
so I know he isn't freezing but I don't know
if he's a he or a she, so I just think he.

He watches doors slide open and closed, open and closed.
So do I.

We look at each other, then back to the doors and I wonder
who will come back first—his owner or my friend?

I watch the doors, then the dog. I watch
two girls walk to their car, chuck frozen A-Treat soda cans
out of the dented trunk, make room for beer.

I look back to the doors, then the dog, and I see
a man in the driver's seat—his owner has come back!
He's won!

But I can't see the dog.
I want to see the dog.

I want to see that he's happy he won,
even though he didn't know there was a contest,
even though he might not be a he,

I want to know he loves his owner, even though
I am assuming all this, I assume things, I assume, I do.

I assume he's a he, I assume his owner loves him,
I assume my friend is coming back,
(milk, she said, just milk).

The man in the truck sits head down, cap down,
rolling a smoke, or checking his phone but
something's not right. I watch.

I see the stripe on what I think is the man's cap
turn into the collar on the dog,
and I realize it's the dog in the truck, not a man in the truck,

it's still the dog, like it's still me, waiting,
only he moved over to the driver's seat. If he's a he.

I've confused a dog and a man. Oh god, I think,
I'm getting carbon monoxide poisoning from a faulty heat vent,

but that's when my friend gets back in the car
with milk, bread, jello, toothpaste, laundry soap.

She begins a story about some guy at the checkout counter
as she backs the car away from the dog
and the truck and the doors and I'm suddenly sad now,

that churned-up-torn-inside-the-chest-feeling sad
because we're leaving and I wish I hadn't won,
I wish he'd won, but he didn't, I won,

and he might not be a he, and I keep twisting, looking
back, hoping for a glimpse of the owner,

but no one's walking toward the dog in the truck
who could get carbon monoxide poisoning,
and there's nothing I can do

but watch as long as I can,
because I need to know that he's all right,
because we were the same back there,
we were the same.

Note to Self

Nothing is where
it should be

inside the rooms
of this house

but the young dog
and the old cat

sprawl side-by-side
contentedly

in their slanted squares
of sunlit air.

How to Move In

Bring in the bed first.
Then the books.
Then wait as long as possible before doing anything else.

Go back to work.
Sweep out the old place.
Volunteer.

Allow time for your books to adjust their spines
in light of a different dust sifting the air
and the deep sighs sounded by floor joists
when no one's there.

Let the books and the light in the room
settle in.
Let the bed be.

Because the promise of sex
is almost as good as sex and sometimes better, let's face it,
so let the bed rest.

The world remains packed with injustice, cockroaches,
pottery shards and implausible physics,
all none of your choosing,

so allow emptiness
to work its little acre
in your life.
Then you'll be home.

Early Morning, Late March

I've been out already,
walking the fields—

winter's high black boots
gleam by the kitchen door

wet and spangled to their tops
with opaque pink blossom.

Thrice

A little wrought iron rosette
on a rooftop door that opens
to mountains and sea
made a bruise shaped like a child's

valentine on my shoulder.
I don't mind.
I ended a fairy tale spell
when I struck it three times

as I carried, first olives,
then cheeses, then a deep rosy wine
to a friend who's come back,
still alive, still alive.

Hard Facts (Defensive Wounds)

She's cleaning fish.
Old rivers of raised veins
twist down her forearms
through networks of scars
down her wrists to the roots
of her fingers, the palms of
her hands, her arms
rest on the workbench a moment,
this woman who could be
any woman on the lee
side of any harbor
where there's been war.
She picks up a bone-handled
blade from the workbench,
scrapes guts into buckets,
flicks bits of shine from her
fingertips, and I wonder
how long, if at all, it took
before she could pick up a knife,
any knife, in her hands cut
by knives, but the answer,
I venture, like the answer
to everything else, is—
it depends on how hungry you get.

Sunflowers after a Storm

Heads bowed in mourning, the big faces
can't countenance what's been flung down
hard and relentless from sky.

Hair neglected, garments muddied,
torn, they stand among the litter,
lacking only black shawls to keen.

But goldfinches hide
in the ripped wide-hearted leaves.
Yellow-black, yellow-black

birds chatter and rise
to the seed-heavy heads.
The coronas crack open and fly.

Old World View

A woman and a man wander
away from the noisy light-strung square,

begin to stroll the narrow street
below my window, carefully now,

aware of the uneven sea-stone cobbles
beneath their feet. The night is warm.

They circle, touch, retreat.
Hands catch, release.

They've been caught in each other's nets.
They become the whole geography—

the sea, fish, wheeling birds,
unyielding shore, salt, heat,

and the ancient, rocky history
of men and women attempting

to storm the high-walled
villages of each other's hearts.

Seaside Retirement

Grandmothers drop the wide straps
of their brassieres and grandfathers
untuck their bright shirts pull them
over their heads like young men at sea's edge
they lie down close their eyes and stretch
out their bodies still bodies still able
to hear waves turn over the beach stones
with satisfied clicks in a sun that's still warm
in October the breezes still light for delicious
long days no one thinks of the children
the lost or the found ones the real or imagined
but of their own mothers and fathers
the sun on their shoulders the moon
on the doorstep the stones in salt water
turn over and over and smaller and smoother.

Dear Passing Thought

You were not an acorn packed with scarlet oak,
a fat burr pulled from a woolen sock

that spurred the invention of Velcro,
not a little rill I followed to a river

that spilled into a rapturous deep sea.
I barely even thought you worth a thought.

You crossed my mind the way,
when I'm not looking, a bird crosses

the rectangle of world outside my window.
How swift, your here-then-gone.

But even though you'll never register
on this day's abacus, I thank you

for the almost-breeze of your almost-touch,
the ease with which you disappear.

A kind of grace, this
never adding up to much.

What's Certain in August

Blackberries, ground fog, and the way old ones
say for every morning's mist this month
there'll be a solid day of snow in February.
Against heat, the dog and I walk early,
leave behind foot-darkened paths and a thousand
silver filaments of broken spider silk.
Such industry from the invisible
spinners and weavers, night after night,
multitudes stitching the solitary things
of the world together, leaf to limb to starry
barb on rusted wire. The dog's out front,
nose down, tail up, tracking what's fresh.
I can't stop looking back. Even this late,
long grasses straighten once we've passed.

Hard Facts (Out Here)

Out here, the roadside bodies,
open-mouthed with twisted throats, are mostly white-tailed
deer, not men, not girls,
not anyone who disagrees.

Sharp bursts of automatic gunfire
from the woods no longer startle me or spook the dogs—
we have no drive-bys,
warlords, ISIL,
Taliban—

just local police at the nearby
outdoor gun range practicing to take down the next shooter
packing hollow points
in high-cap magazines
who walks into

a school, church, café,
hotel, nightclub, shopping mall.
Late light ignites pale purple
arcs of raspberry
at field's edge,

on cue, a single slender
egret rises from the marsh to disappear in trees
and makes things briefly right.
We sit out side-by-side,
watch night come on.

4

Changes to Your Itinerary May Affect Your Fate

That's what I read on my train ticket. But my ticket says
fare, not *fate*, it says *Changes to Your Itinerary*

May Affect your Fare, and the ticket doesn't actually say
anything; it isn't even a ticket; it's a barcode

composed of light and dark patterns attached to four pages
of wasted ink on wasted wood pulp, flattened and chemically

bleached into blinding white paper sheets at the peril
of our drinking water, outlining precisely

how few legal rights I retain specific to my journey
by rail between Washington D.C. and New York City

today, a changeable day, that started fogged in, began to
burn off near the Susquehanna River where the train takes

flight above the water's wide shine, once
represented with aluminum foil between two banks

of green-dyed play-dough in my 4th grade geography project
entitled "Colonial Waterways" (B+, Try to be neater).

As we cross the high trestle over yet another river
that didn't lead to the fragrant spice markets of India,

I see these ticket pages are filled with fat chunks
of small-fonted language footnoted by stars, double stars

and crosses, outlining the rules for baggage,
our considerable baggage, what we carry with us,

jammed into overhead compartments or clogging the aisles,
rules about money and stuff, but nothing about fate

or its three badass goddesses who spin, measure, cut out
the length of a life and nothing about what we drag behind us

freighted with denials of the past like long cotton collecting bags
pulled down dark rows by dark bodies, but even if it were

about fate, even if I switch trains, head to Pittsburgh
on the Pennsylvanian where the brass plaque

at the confluence of the westward rolling Ohio River
says Fort Pitt's capture from the French and Indians

in 1758 *established Anglo-Saxon Supremacy in the United States*—
it's hard to misread *Anglo-Saxon Supremacy* no matter

what direction one turns, none of which (including
smallpox infected blankets) is touched on in the fine print

contained by this sheaf of papers masquerading as a ticket
which I know now has nothing to do with fate—

(go ask Oedipus, Iphigenia, or the two men
who survived the collapse of the World Trade towers

but died in the Staten Island Ferry crash, ask them
about fate)—I just read it that way, because

I'm stupidly hopeful for answers and I could have misread
fare as *fade* or *fame* or *face* or *hate*

because Changes to Your Itinerary May Affect Your Face
is also true, as is Changes to Your Itinerary May Affect

Your Hate, a thing screaming from my newspaper
this morning so hard that I read

(and then misread) my ticket's disclaimer instead.
I'm trying to take heart. I am trying to take heart

in the wrong words by turning them
into the right ones. It's not working.

But I'm trying. I'm quieting down now, taking a cue
from the lawyers in the wide cushy seats

of the first class car who know
all the business resides in the conditional case—

packed tight with the power of might,
in the smart snappy briefcase of *may*.

Possibilities for Roadside Theatre

There's the rump-sprung sofa in its kudzu-draped parlor
off Route 29, a rusted folding chair and upturned
milk crate at the apple orchard's edge
where an old man sat in every kind of weather

until one day he didn't, which is one way
these small shows end. On River Road, a two-toned
car seat tilted back for speed surveys fishing skiffs
and flotsam near a picnic table no one uses,

and today an oxblood leather wingchair studded
with dull rivets made its debut on the highway shoulder
where I turn for home and what to make of this?
I stop my car, investigate. Divorce or infestation?

Ink-stained, soiled, a seat someone never liked?
Or simply worn, rejected, its torn back turned now
to the setting sun? I decide to take my place
in today's oddball entre'acte and I stand beside it,

consort posing with the throne. Our shadows
stretch before us across concrete, and cars travel
through our long flat figures (woman, chair) in a slurry
of blurred faces. Only the children wave back.

I Need to Live Near a Creek

because
the lush

mossy
rush of it

hushes
me up.

Accrual

Some nights my mind still tries
to peel away squares of blackened paper
from the old-fashioned kiosk

of my spinal column, photographs
and placards posted by the body
behind the mind's back, years ago,

glued with spit and wheat paste.
Images gone, titles gone,
all part of the whole

structure now, hardened,
darkened, their weight subsumed
into frame. The way a tree grows

first around, then through, barbed
wire, or folds the small grey marble
headstone of a child into its

knotted roots. Such heaviness
our bones haul in and hold inside.
No wonder we can't fly.

Thunderstorm

Aching for body like the old days
      and bored with parading
            stately cloud ships
            through blazing blue skies,
      the gods seize any chance they can muster

to tumble from terrible heights,
      smash down hard into sidewalks and highways
            with head-banging explosions
            that rise into small perfect
      clear-beaded crowns

that shatter and rush through jammed
      storm drains and culverts
            to join the communion of rivers,
            or they fall for the thrill
      of the wind once again

like peregrine falcons and long-skirted women
      on desolate moors,
            slashing cornfields and hayfields
            in vaporous curtains
      that catch tassel tips,

seed head and broadleaf,
      condense into droplets that ride
            cool down green stems
            and segmented stalks
      to delicate underworld roots

where they linger and relish
the deliciously ruddy,
dark, crumbling
chocolate
of earth. Then they rise.

Hard Facts (Especially)

Most everything we're taught
is wrong.

Especially fixed rules
about small engine

repair in adverse
marine conditions,

walking on ice,
and anything

to do with people.
Especially our own

strange selves.
And so the door

to the ordinary miracle
swings open.

Unexpected Ocean Voyage

That arched blue
doorway curls beneath
a wooden lintel
like a great wave lifting
an ancient ship
out to sea
carried by a spinnaker
of scarlet bougainvillea
rigged and rooted
to a terracotta pot.

In the Straw Market

Under two battered trees,
I bought the first basket offered,
paid what was asked.

I did not hold its belly to the light,
check stitch or weave
or seams or yoke, did not
fret its simple design.
I had not been taught what to seek.

And yet, just today,
the basket cradled
three ripe cantaloupes
and ten small limes,
mixed their perfumes
with a woody bottom note
of dried palmetto,

strong handles looped
over my shoulder,
ten years later,
all the long way home.

Shape Shifting

Windows wide open to night's end,
last hot breath of summer.
Maybe you've never heard this song,
how the screech owl sounds
like a horse's whinny
slight wind sifting through a sycamore
precisely like another
sleep-scented body shifting in its sleep,
how those glugs and whirrs
from the amphibious
crowd at marsh and creek
match the murmurs and leaps
of your own underwater heart.
Every single thing's
like every other single thing—
beneath skin, exoskeleton, carapace,
we might even be each other—
were we only sound.

Losing It with Nature

I've had it with turkey vultures
perched like black lungs
hung in the bone-white branches of the buttonwood;

and I've had it with the buttonwood tree
that plays dead
into June then coughs fat leaves to life in time

to drop them burnt brown first thing
every fall when vultures
like to gather on the barn roof, hold their jagged

wings above their naked scrotum heads
in awful benediction;
I've had it with the scientific explanation for this

(drying feathers, regulating body temperature)
because I know
a bad sign when I see one as these years fill up

with slaughter. I clap hands, flap arms,
watch the bastards
barely even turn their beaks to cast a hooded eye

at me, and it's exactly because I know I'm being foolish
that I start screaming
which brings the dog, who's always game, who tells me

with a look she's had it too. She's howling, I'm screaming,
and we're scrambling
up the bank as I chuck leathery chartreuse walnuts

at the barn's tin roof—*bam!bam!bam!*—
until the vultures drop
their headless horseman capes, begin to beat the air

with silver-black, loose-feathered wings
and we fall back
exhausted, satisfied, because we sure showed them.

Once

She saw it all
on an ordinary morning
from her porch

in the clear glass
globe of a bird feeder,
thrum

of a single
ruby-throated
hummingbird

taking long drinks of sugar water
from red trumpets
flaring below,

and she was in it
too, inside the glass,
all of her,

her scarlet bathrobe,
solid house and door
behind her,

roof, trees, street,
the town she had adopted,
white sky, heartbeat

whir—all of it
reflected in nectar, then all gone.

Retirement Speech for Fear

Fear, being first to enter the body,
      wants to be last to leave.
It needs to check deadbolts, door locks,
      motion sensors, shine flashlight beams
down stairwells, arm alarms with secret code.
      Fear can't help but be nostalgic
for the years it ran the whole show here—
      the way it wiped out everything before,
how with a single creak inside a house,
      a dried leaf skittering along the street,
a sonic boom, a buckle click, a scent,
      it seized up the core machinery,
made workers cower underneath their desks
      brought black-clad SWAT teams
spilling out of armored cars,
      powered by the limbic brain.
And all this several times a day for years.
      It goes to one's head, to own a body's country
so completely. Fear's fierce, familiar grip
      that says *belong to me or die,*
sure feels a lot like love. But here we are today
      to say good-bye, send fear away
to well-deserved retirement,
      grateful for the echo of its work shoes
on the body's polished corridors.
      Let's have all systems rise
with thunderous applause for fear
      who's served us well. We won't forget.
We stand and wait, we know the way
      this works. We watch fear pause

at the door to pat its pocket,
    touch the reassuring metal outline
of the body's master key.
    We know fear won't go far.

Epiphany with Trashcans, Ice Pond, and Four Hemlocks

Late-day-tired, I look up
from dragging trash cans down the lane

to gauge how much light is left to finish
what's never finished:

firewood, garbage, sweepings, ash,
as an unremarkable low flat cloud takes light

dead west in the bone-ache cold of a winter afternoon,
begins to climb its own body, crystal

by frozen crystal, builds itself up
into a steep-peaked mountain from a Chinese print

above my neighbor's ice pond with its quartet
of black-spined hemlocks already stocked with night.

I wait silently with them, watch the day's last fire pour out
cold and straight across

what little we are made of—
water vapor, temperature, hard clean curve of stone.

So little and so much.
It sums us up.

Acknowledgments

Grateful acknowledgment is made to the editors of the following journals in which these poems first appeared, some in altered form:

Blue Heron Review: "Sunflowers after a Storm"
Cider Press Review: "How to Move In"
Odyssey: "Seaside Retirement," "Thrice," "Unexpected Ocean Voyage," "World View"
Philadelphia Stories: "Changes to Your Itinerary May Affect Your Fate"
Poet Lore: "Performing Heart Repair Surgery at 2 A.M. While Asleep," "Riverside Attractions/Terminal Avenue"
Rattle: "Hard Facts (Do Not Resist)," "How It Is with My Father"
Schuylkill Valley Journal: "Deep Run," "Her Eulogy, As If Composed by the Moon," "Nostalgia," "Shape Shifting," "That Winter"
Southern Poetry Review: "Adage," "To a Passing Thought"
Tar River Poetry: "Early Morning, Late March," "What's Certain in August"
U.S. 1 Worksheets: "Dear Friend Since Childhood," "Once," "Sometimes the Journey's All in Your Head"
Virginia Quarterly Review: "Bitter Night in the Country"
The Wagon: "At the Straw Market," "Dear T, Who Overdosed," "Note to Self," "Small Wish for Your Last Breaths"

My thanks to Christopher Bursk and Luray Gross for early manuscript reading and to all who offered thoughts on individual poems, particularly the Montco Wordshop and the

Pinkers for varied perspectives, and to the poetry community of Bucks County for their wide and constant support.

I am deeply grateful to Diane Lockward and Terrapin Books for steady editorial guidance and belief in this book.

Special thanks to my sister Abby Brooks for showing up with the right stuff at the right time and to Reb, Sam, and Abby, for always. And thank you again Reb, because I can never thank you enough.

About the Author

Hayden Saunier is the author of three poetry collections, *Tips for Domestic Travel*, *Say Luck*, which won the 2013 Gell Poetry Prize, and *Field Trip to the Underworld*, winner of the Keystone Chapbook Award. Her work has been awarded the Pablo Neruda Prize, the Rattle Poetry Prize, and the Robert Fraser Award. She has been published in a variety of journals, including *Beloit Poetry Journal*, *Drunken Boat*, *Nimrod*, *The Virginia Quarterly Review*, and *Tar River Poetry*. She holds an MFA from the Bennington Writing Seminars, is a professional actress and teaching artist, and lives on a farm in Bucks County, Pennsylvania.

CPSIA information can be obtained
at www.ICGtesting.com
Printed in the USA
BVOW08s0310200617

487338BV00003B/6/P